# Nature's Children

## STICK INSECTS

### Geoff Miller

High Meadows School
Library Media Center
1055 Willeo Road
Roswell, GA 30075

# FACTS IN BRIEF

**Classification of Stick Insects**

Class: *Insecta* (insects)
Subclass: *Pterygota*
Order: *Phasmida* (stick and leaf insects)
Family: *Phasmatidae* (stick insect family)
Species: There are about 2,000 species of stick insects.

**World distribution.** Worldwide. More common in tropical and subtropical regions.

**Habitat.** Any area where plants are plentiful, especially tropical rain forests.

**Distinctive physical characteristics.** Sticklike bodies; spindly legs; green, gray, or brown in color; some types grow to 12 inches (30 centimeters) in length.

**Habits.** Conceal themselves among leaves and stems. Active mainly at night. Remain motionless for long periods. Lay hundreds of seedlike eggs.

**Diet.** Stick insects feed exclusively on plants.

---

All rights reserved. Except for use in a review, no part of this book may be reproduced, stored in a retrieval system, or transmitted in any form, or by any means, electronic, mechanical photocopying, recording, or otherwise, without prior permission of the publisher.

© 1999 Brown Partworks Limited
Printed and bound in U.S.A.
Editor: James Kinchen
Designer: Tim Brown

**Published by:**

GROLIER EDUCATIONAL

Sherman Turnpike, Danbury, Connecticut 06816

**Library of Congress Cataloging-in-Publishing Data**

Stick Insects.
   p. cm. -- (Nature's children. Set 6)
   ISBN 0-7172-9368-8 (alk. paper) -- ISBN 0-7172-9351-3 (set)
   1. Stick Insects--Juvenile Literature. [1. Stick Insects.] I. Grolier Educational (Firm) II. Series.

QL509.5.M55  1999
595.7'29—dc21

98-33408

# Contents

| | |
|---|---|
| Stick Insect Territory | Page 6 |
| Abundant Insects | Page 9 |
| Sticks and Leaves | Page 10 |
| Body Parts | Page 13 |
| Suits of Armor | Page 14 |
| Drawing Breath | Page 17 |
| Masters of Disguise | Page 18 |
| Stick Insect Mealtime | Page 21 |
| Insect Wings | Page 22 |
| Flying Sticks | Page 25 |
| Keen Senses | Page 26 |
| Hanging Around | Page 29 |
| Two Kinds of Reproduction | Page 30 |
| Laying Eggs | Page 33 |
| Stick Insect Eggs | Page 34 |
| Hatching Out | Page 36 |
| Growing Up | Page 37 |
| Regeneration | Page 41 |
| Staying Safe | Page 42 |
| Fighting Back | Page 45 |
| Vanishing Sticks | Page 46 |
| Words to Know | Page 47 |
| Index | Page 48 |

Almost everywhere you go in the world, you will come across insects. Flies, butterflies, beetles, ants, ladybugs, bees, wasps, and dragonflies are just a few of the many kinds you might see. There are more than 1 million different types, or species, of insects, and new ones are discovered by scientists every year.

Insects have been around for hundreds of millions of years. During this time they have changed, or adapted, themselves so that they can survive in many different environments. Stick insects, as their name suggests, actually look like twigs or small branches. With their slender, twiglike bodies they can safely hide in bushes and trees. Over millions of years these insects have adapted themselves to suit their conditions so that now they look like the plants on which they live.

*With its twiglike body the stick insect can cleverly disguise itself as part of a plant.*

## Stick Insect Territory

If you want to see stick insects in the wild, the best places to go are in the tropics. The tropics are the parts of the world nearest to the equator, where it is hot and sunny all year round. Stick insects are particularly abundant in the rain forests of Africa, Asia, and South America, where there are plenty of fresh plants for them to eat. However, tropical forests are not the only places where stick insects live—you can also find them in North America, Australia, and the warmer parts of Europe around the Mediterranean Sea.

*This stick insect lives in the Amazon rain forest in South America.*

## Abundant Insects

Insects are the most successful of all creatures. Almost two-thirds of the earth's animals are insects. There are at least 2,000 species of stick insects. To help sort out the different types of insects, scientists place them into large groups called orders. The group to which the stick insects belong is called Phasmida, which comes from a Greek word meaning "having a strange appearance." This name refers to the stick insects' ability to look like the branches on which they live.

Insects come in a great range of sizes, some are almost too small to see, while others grow to be 14-inch-long (35-centimeter) giants. Stick insects are among the biggest insects. Adult stick insects usually measure from three to six inches (eight to 15 centimeters) in length, but the largest can be one foot (30 centimeters) long.

*If this giant stick insect sat on your arm, it would stretch from your fingertips to beyond your elbow.*

## Sticks and Leaves

The stick insect family includes stick insects and their close relatives, the leaf insects. Stick insects get their name from their spindly bodies. They stay for many hours in the same spot without moving, blending perfectly with the plants on which they live. Leaf insects are just as remarkable, and as you might have guessed, they do a magnificent impression of a leaf. It can be an intriguing sight to see what you thought was just another leaf suddenly begin to walk. They are so well disguised that other insects, even other leaf insects, sometimes take a bite out of them by mistake! Leaf insects are found in most of the places where stick insects live, particularly in the tropical rain forests.

*This Japanese leaf insect imitates both the color and shape of a leaf.*

## Body Parts

Although there is a huge variety of insect types, they all have the same basic body structure. The word *insect* means "in sections" and accurately describes the way their bodies are formed. If you look very carefully at an insect, you will notice that its body is made up of three separate parts: the head, the thorax, or middle section, and the abdomen, or rear.

Stick insects have long, slim bodies so that they can hide themselves among the trees and branches. Not all types of stick insects have wings, but those that do have slender, delicate wings. These are kept folded back along their bodies to maintain their sticklike disguises. The longest part of a stick insect's body is its abdomen, which is divided into smaller segments. The segments are joined by flexible joints that let the stick insect bend its body.

*By carefully placing its legs so they blend naturally with the twig, a stick insect makes its disguise even more effective.*

## Suits of Armor

Inside our bodies we have a framework of bones called a skeleton. Around this are our muscles and skin. Insects do not have a bony skeleton on the inside like us. Instead, they have a strong outer casing that surrounds their bodies like a suit of armor. An insect's outer skeleton is made up of many sections of tough material fitted together with bendy joints to allow for movement.

Every so often during its life a stick insect needs to molt, or shed, its outer covering so that it can grow. The insect grows a new skeleton underneath the old one. Then the old skin cracks open, letting the newly covered insect emerge. The new outer casing is soft at first, and the insect must take care to avoid danger until it hardens.

*This close-up photograph of a spiny stick insect reveals a rather frightening face!*

## Drawing Breath

If you look closely at the cast-off skin of a stick insect, you may notice some very fine threads hanging from the inside of the casing. These strange threads give us a clue as to how insects breathe.

Like all animals, insects must breathe in oxygen from the air to live, but unlike humans, insects do not have lungs. An insect breathes air into its body through a number of tiny openings called spiracles. A stick insect has 10 pairs of these holes along its body—two on its thorax and the rest along its abdomen. The holes connect up to a network of fine tubes that carry the oxygen to where it is needed in the insect's body. The fine, shiny threads left hanging from the stick insect's discarded outer casing are actually the remains of its old set of breathing tubes!

*Holding onto the bottom of a leaf, a stick insect creeps out of its old outer casing.*

## Masters of Disguise

When soldiers go into battle, they often disguise themselves to fool their enemies or to make themselves difficult to see. The patchy colors on their uniforms and vehicles, called camouflage, help them to blend in with their surroundings. Animals also use disguise to hide from predators. With their twig-shaped bodies stick insects are masters of disguise and can be almost impossible to pick out from the surrounding plants. Colored green, gray, or reddish brown, they are very difficult to spot amongst leaves and branches. A stick insect can also remain almost still for hours at a time, looking exactly like a plant's stem. Sometimes when a breeze blows, it will sway gently backward and forward to complete its masterful disguise.

*Can you spot the stick insect hiding on this moss-covered branch?*

## Stick Insect Mealtime

Stick insects spend most of their time living among trees and bushes, and their favorite foods are the leaves and stems of plants. Unlike many insects, which catch and eat other creatures for food, stick insects are purely vegetarian—they eat only plants. They feed mostly during the night and particularly enjoy fresh, green leaves and tender shoots. Stick insects use their powerful jaws, called mandibles, to munch their food. Some species eat only one type of plant, while others are not so choosy and will eat many different types.

    Stick insects have big appetites. Sometimes they gather together in large groups called swarms. A single swarm has been known to strip trees completely bare of their leaves.

*This stick insect, from Argentina in South America, is nibbling on a blade of grass.*

## Insect Wings

Insect wings are as varied as the insects themselves—think of the beautiful wings of a butterfly or the long, delicate wings of a dragonfly. Not all insects are able to fly, but those that can have either one or two pairs of wings. Some do not have any at all, such as most types of ants. Stick insects are unusual because some species have wings, while others do not.

Most insect wings are thin and light and look almost transparent. A network of tubes, called veins, running down the wings makes them rigid and strong. Insects such as flies and wasps have only a few veins running down their wings, while other insects, such as dragonflies, have intricate patterns that crisscross their wings. Experts can tell a lot about different insects by studying the patterns on their wings.

*A stick insect flutters its strong but light wings.*

*Stay away! A stick insect opens its wings as a warning to frighten predators away.*

24

# Flying Sticks

Stick insects that can fly have two pairs of wings. Usually the front wings are not very large, and the rear pair is more important for flying. The wings are joined to the stick insect's body at its thorax. When they are not in use, a stick insect keeps its wings tucked away beside its body. In this position the front edges of the wings look a little like withered leaves. The undersides of some stick insects' wings are brightly colored. If the insect is attacked, the wings can be quickly unfolded to reveal a bright flash of color that may scare the predator away.

    Stick insects are not especially good flyers. Sometimes instead of using its wings to fly, a stick insect may use them like miniature parachutes. If it is disturbed by a predator, it falls from its branch, unfolds its wings, and glides safely to the ground.

## Keen Senses

To discover what is going on around them, stick insects have eyes and antennae. Insect eyes are not the same as human eyes. Like many insects, stick insects have compound eyes, which are made up of thousands of tiny lenses. Compound eyes enable insects to see movement in all directions at the same time—almost as if they have eyes in the back of their heads. Each tiny lens adds to the overall picture that the stick insect sees. Some types of stick insects have several other eyes, too. These "simple" eyes are not as advanced as their compound eyes. They pick up only basic information such as color and brightness.

As well as having excellent eyes, a stick insect has antennae that look like two little aerials at the front of its head. Tiny hairs covering the antennae pick up chemical signals in the air and also help the insect to keep its balance.

*Notice the large compound eye and the two long antennae on this giant prickly stick insect's head.*

## Hanging Around

Unlike grasshoppers and crickets, most stick insects cannot jump or leap. They are slow-moving creatures, which helps to explain why they need to disguise themselves so well. If they were easily seen, they would soon be attacked and eaten by faster-moving predators.

A stick insect moves its three pairs of legs slowly and carefully along the leaves and branches. Once a good resting place has been found, it often hangs in what looks like a dangerous position—jutting out stiffly into the air. Stick insects can hold on and stay in these difficult positions because they have little claws and special sticky pads on their feet. Some stick insects that live near streams can cling tightly to rocks while fast-flowing water washes over them.

*Safely hidden from predators, a stick insect hangs onto a tree with its sticky pads and tiny claws.*

## Two Kinds of Reproduction

Stick insects are unusual because, depending on the species, they reproduce in two quite different ways. In some species all of the insects are females. A special process allows their eggs to develop without being fertilized by a male. In other species there are both male and female stick insects. When it is old enough to breed, the male goes in search of a suitable female partner. To mate, the male climbs onto the female's back and curves his slim abdomen around hers. Mating pairs have sometimes been seen locked together in the same position for several hours while the male fertilizes the female's eggs.

*A much smaller male stick insect sits on top of the female to fertilize her eggs.*

## Laying Eggs

About two weeks after mating, the female stick insect is ready to lay her eggs. She lays them through a special tube at the tip of her abdomen called an ovipositor. Many types of stick insect simply drop their eggs onto the ground, but the females of some species are more careful and deliberate. Some bury their eggs or hide them in cracks in the bark of a tree. Others even attach their eggs to leaves or branches with a special gluey substance that oozes from their bodies.

Some species have a more spectacular method of laying eggs—they flick, or catapult, them over a wide area. The female suspends herself upside down from a branch and arches her abdomen before straightening up to throw the eggs to the ground some distance away.

*A female stick insect searches for a safe crack in the bark of a tree where she can lay her eggs.*

## Stick Insect Eggs

Stick insects lay a great number of eggs, often as many as 200. The eggs come in a variety of shapes and sizes, depending on the species. The smallest eggs are about the same size as the head of a pin, while the largest are less than half an inch (one centimeter) long—roughly the size of a fingernail.

All stick insect eggs have a very tough outer shell for protection. They look a bit like seeds or tiny nuts. Some eggs are shiny and smooth, while others are textured with intricate patterns. At one end of the egg there is a tiny cap, or lid, from which the baby stick insect will eventually emerge. A minute hole at the other end lets moisture and air into the egg, allowing the baby stick insect to breathe and develop inside.

*A baby stick insect will hatch through the lid of each of these nutlike eggs.*

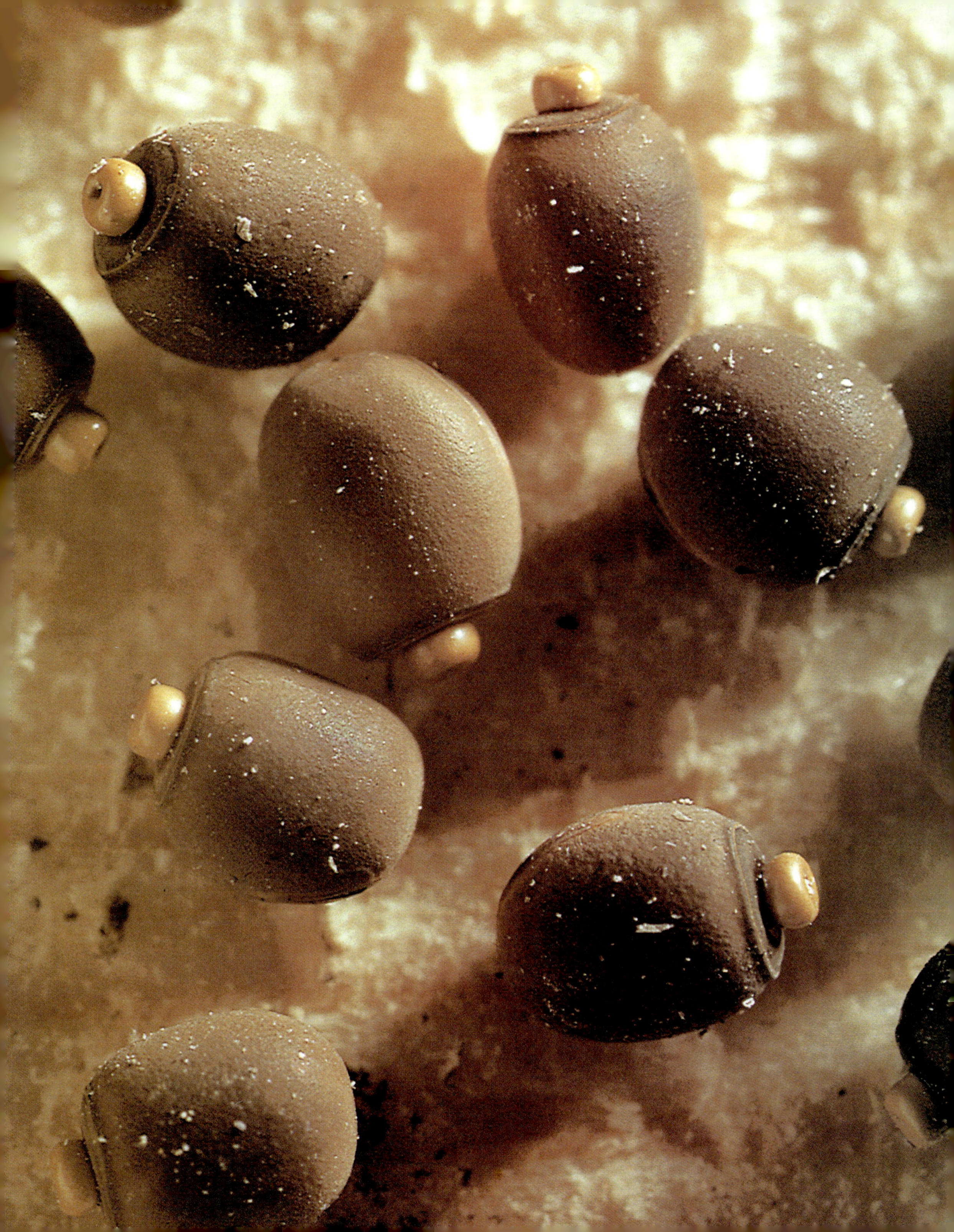

## Hatching Out

It can take a long time for stick insect eggs to hatch out—from four to eight months. Throughout this time the baby stick insect is growing and developing inside the egg.

If you have ever seen a baby chick hatching, you know that it smashes open its eggshell. However, when a stick insect hatches, it simply pushes off the egg's special lid and climbs out through the opening. It breaks free of the egg by pulling itself out headfirst and hauling the rest of its body after it. Inside its egg a baby stick insect lies tightly coiled up like a spring, but on emerging it stretches out its body and may be as much as eight times as long as its eggshell!

# Growing Up

Young stick insects are known as nymphs and are born into the world as almost perfect copies of their parents. Over the next three to six months the youngster sheds, or molts, its skin several times, growing each time it molts until it becomes an adult. Every time it changes its skin, the insect almost doubles in size. Some stick insects' bodies are covered with spines to deter predators, and these, too, grow larger each time the nymph molts.

In those stick insect species that have wings, the wings first appear as little buds on the sides of the nymph's body. Only when all the stages have been completed are the wings fully formed.

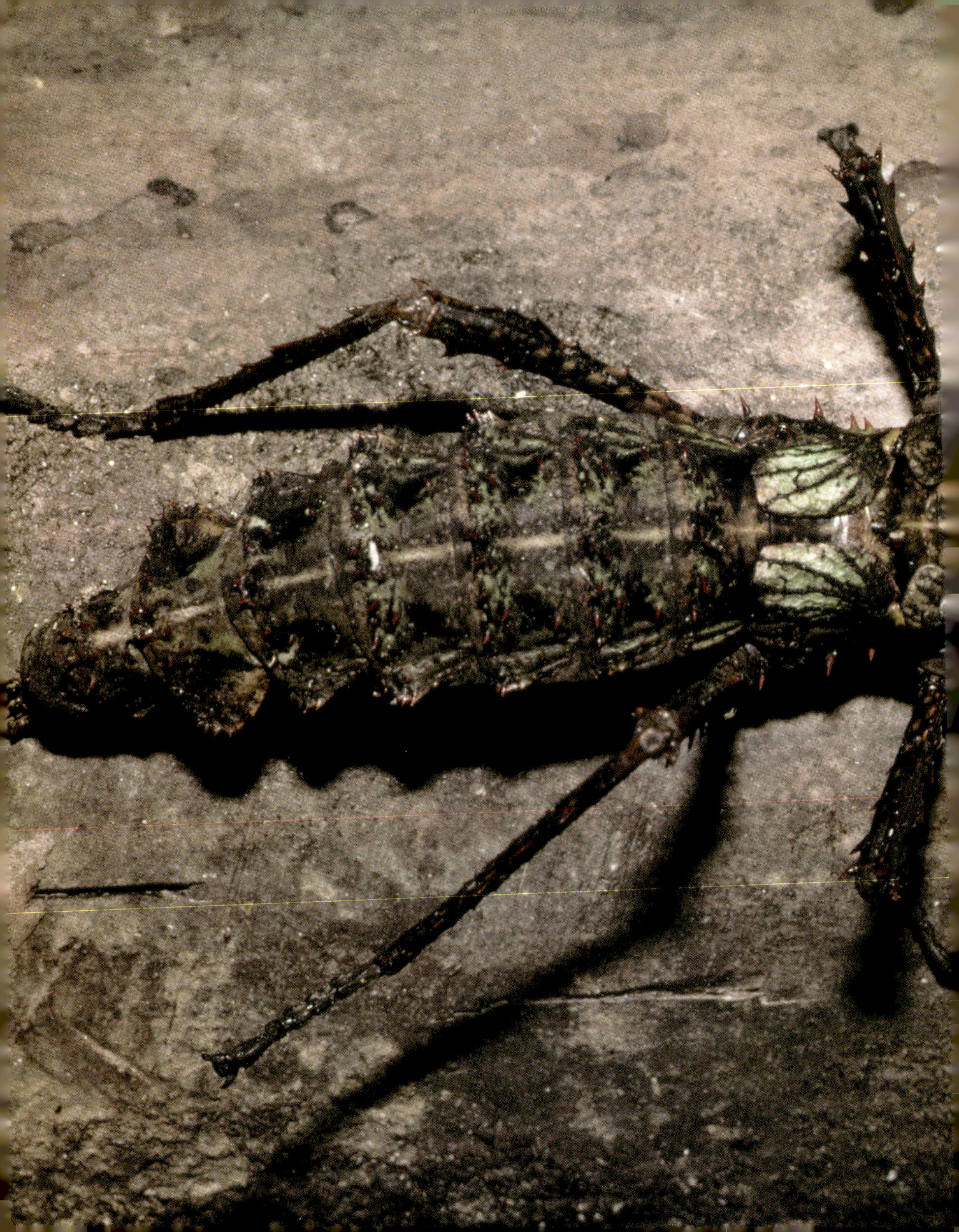

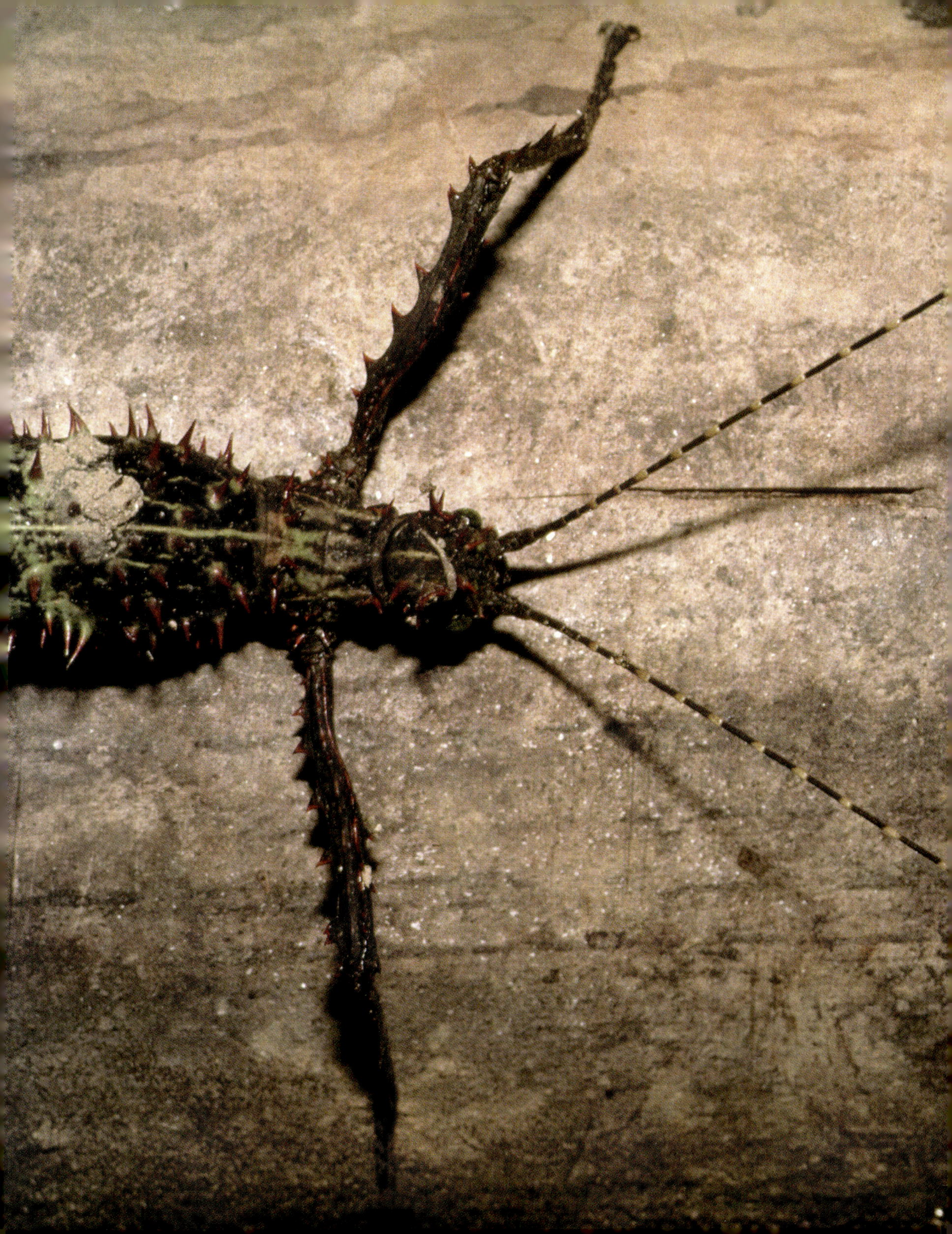

*How many times has this stick insect lost a leg? As a nymph, it may have lost and regrown more than one of its legs!*

# Regeneration

As well as developing its wings and spines, a young stick insect can even regenerate, or regrow, a lost leg when changing its skin. Imagine being able to grow a new leg or arm! If attacked by a predator, the stick insect can give up a healthy leg in order to escape. Each time the insect molts, the lost limb will gradually grow back. After three or four molts a new limb will have grown to replace the one that was lost. The new limb never quite grows to full size and will always be slightly shorter than the original. If the insect loses one of its antennae, this, too, can be replaced. Instead of growing another antenna, however, another leg appears in its place! When stick insects reach adult size, they no longer molt, so only nymphs can replace body parts in this way.

## Staying Safe

In the wild stick insects are in danger of being eaten by lizards, birds, and spiders. Because they are not very fast or aggressive creatures, stick insects have developed other ways to stay safe from predators. Their best form of defense is, of course, not to be noticed in the first place. Their ability to look like the twigs and stems of the plants they live on is a great way of keeping a low profile. Stick insects are active mostly during the night and spend the daylight hours sitting motionless in trees and bushes.

In addition to their ability to stay unnoticed, many stick insects have strong, sharp spines on the outside of their bodies. These spines will injure any enemy that tries to gobble them up.

*Keep off! Spines on the body of this young Australian stick insect help protect it from hungry predators.*

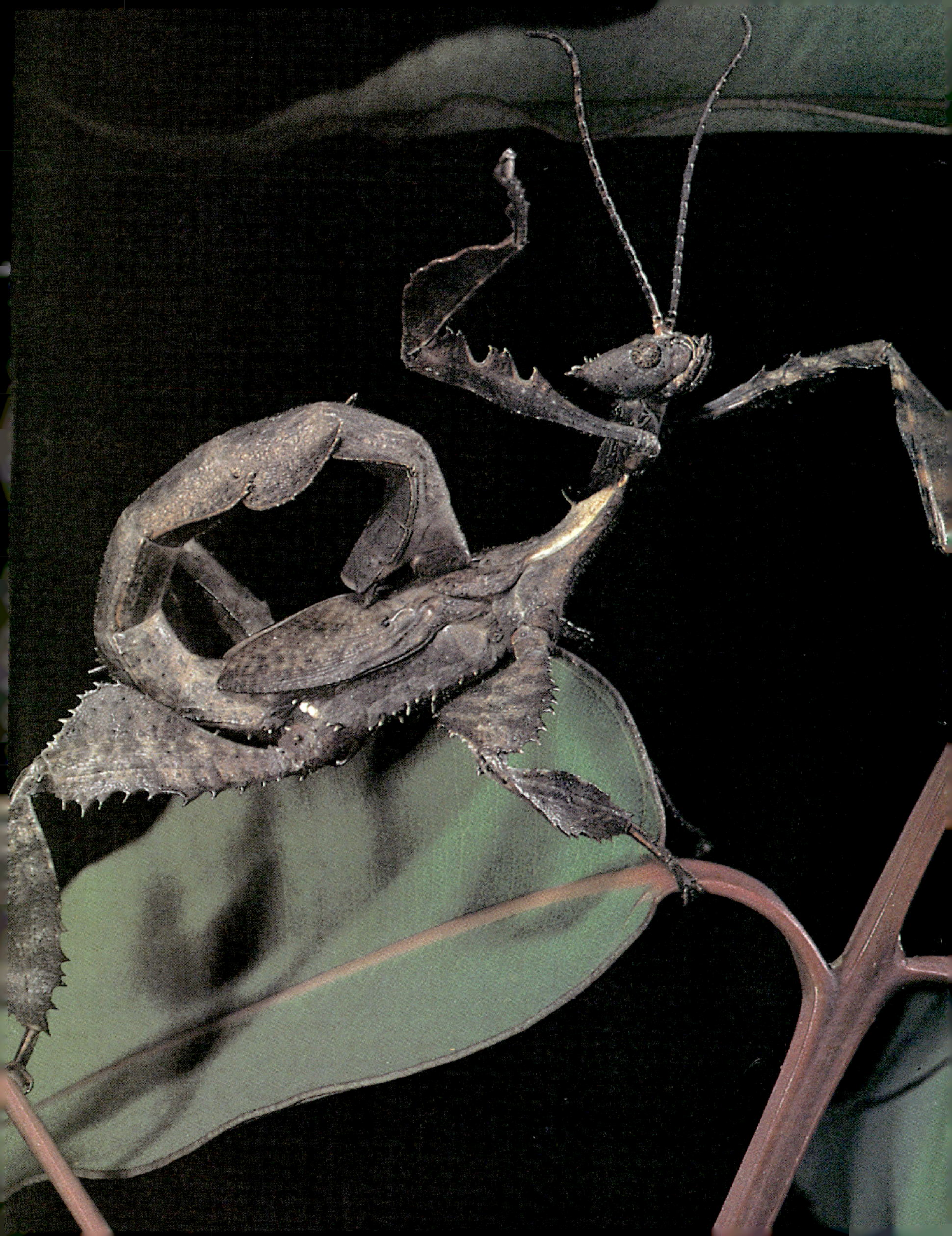

*This great spiny stick insect curls its tail like a scorpion—a fearsome sight to any attacker.*

## Fighting Back

Although their main defense against possible predators is their camouflage, stick insects also defend themselves in other ways. They often try to surprise an attacker with a display of sudden, unexpected behavior. One way they do this is to curl their long tails over their backs like scorpions. Another way is to suddenly show a bright flash of color from under their wings. Other stick insects will quickly twist and tumble, dropping to the ground and lying motionless, pretending to be dead. Often they will remain like this for hours, until they are certain that the hunter has moved away.

If all else fails, some stick insects can produce a foul-smelling liquid. Some spray the liquid at enemies, scaring or even blinding them. Others cover themselves with the liquid, making their bodies smell unpleasant.

## Vanishing Sticks

While stick insects are very good at avoiding their natural enemies, some human activities pose a serious threat to these masters of disguise. In many areas farmers spray chemicals called insecticides onto their crops to protect them from harmful insects. These chemicals can remain in the environment for years and kill many innocent insects, including stick insects.

The biggest threat to stick insects, however, is the destruction of their homes. All over the world woodlands and rain forests are being cut down to make space for human development. As the trees and bushes disappear, so do the stick insects.

# Words to Know

**Abdomen**  The rear part of an insect's body that contains the stomach and parts used to lay eggs.

**Antennae**  Feelers on top of an insect's head that are used for smelling, touching, and tasting.

**Camouflage**  Patterns or colors that help an animal to blend in to its surroundings and not be seen by predators.

**Compound eyes**  Large eyes found on many insects. Each is made up of many lenses.

**Equator**  An imaginary circle around the earth, midway between the North and South Poles.

**Mandibles**  The sharp cutting parts of an insect's mouth.

**Molt**  To shed an old skin to make way for a larger one.

**Nymph**  Young insect.

**Ovipositor**  A female insect's egg-laying tube.

**Predator**  An animal that hunts and eats other animals for food.

**Spiracles**  Tiny holes in an insect's body case for taking in air.

**Thorax**  The middle part of an insect's body that holds the wings and legs.

# INDEX

abdomen, 13, 17, 30, 33, 47
antennae, 26, 27, 41, 47; *illus.*, 27
Australian stick insect, 42;
  *illus.*, 43

body shape, 5, 10, 13, 18, 36
breathing, 17, 34

camouflage, 18, 45, 47

defense, 25, 42, 44, 45; *illus.*, 44
development, 34, 36, 37

eggs, 30, 33, 34, 36; *illus.*, 35
  laying, 33; *illus.*, 32
equator, 6, 47
eyes, 26, 27, 47; *illus.*, 27

feeding, 21; *illus.*, 20
flying, 22, 25

giant prickly stick insect, 27;
  *illus.*, 27
giant stick insect, 9; *illus.*, 8
great spiny stick insect, 44;
  *illus.*, 44

head, 13, 26
hiding, 5, 10, 13, 18, 29, 42;
  *illus.*, 12, 19

leaf insect, 10; *illus.*, 11
legs, 29, 40, 41

mandibles, 21, 47
mating, 30, 33; *illus.*, 31
molt, 14, 17, 37, 41, 47; *illus.*, 16
movement, 14, 18, 26, 29

nymph, 37, 40, 41, 47

ovipositor, 33, 47

predators, 24, 29, 37, 41, 42, 45, 47

rain forest, 6, 10, 46
regeneration, 41

senses, 26
size, 9, 37
skeleton, 14
spines, 37, 41, 42; *illus.*, 43
spiny stick insect, 14; *illus.*, 15
spiracles, 17, 47

thorax, 13, 17, 25, 47

wings, 13, 22, 24, 25, 37, 41, 45;
  *illus.*, 23, 24

young stick insect, 34, 37

**Cover Photo:** Michael Fogden & Patricia Fogden / Corbis
**Photo Credits:** Geoff Moon; FLPA / Corbis, page 4; Michael Fogden & Patricia Fogden / Corbis, page 7; Buddy Mays / Corbis, pages 8, 31, 40; Ron Austing; FLPA / Corbis, page 11; Stephen Dalton / NHPA, pages 12, 35; Robert Pickett / Corbis, page 15; Anthony Bannister; ABPL / Corbis, page 16; G. I. Bernard / NHPA, pages 19, 23; Joe McDonald / Corbis, page 20; Stephen Krasemann / NHPA, page 24; Michael Leach / NHPA, page 27; B. Borell Casals; FLPA / Corbis, page 28; Wolfgang Kaehler / Corbis, page 32; Chris Hellier / Corbis, page 38; Pavel German / NHPA, page 43; Chris Mattison; FLPA / Corbis, page 44.

| DATE DUE | | | |
|---|---|---|---|
| | | | |
| | | | |
| | | | |
| | | | |
| | | | |
| | | | |
| | | | |
| | | | |
| | | | |
| | | | |
| | | | |
| | | | |
| | | | |